Bilingual Picture Dictionaries

My First Book of
French
Words

by Katy R. Kudela

Translator: Translations.com

apple
la pomme
(pom)

raintree

...any — publishers for children

Contents

How to use this dictionary

This book is full of useful words in both French and English. The English word appears first, followed by the French word. Look below each French word for help to sound it out. Try reading the words aloud.

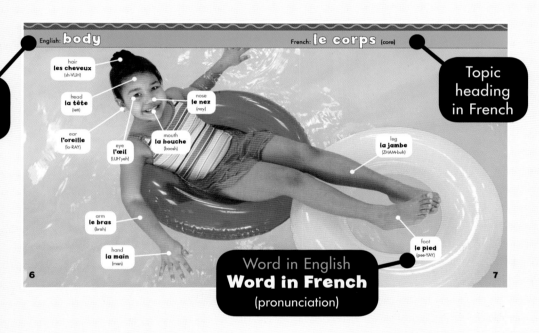

Topic heading in English

Topic heading in French

Word in English
Word in French
(pronunciation)

English: **body**

French: **le corps** (core)

hair
les cheveux
(sh-VUH)

head
la tête (tett)

nose
le nez (nay)

ear
l'oreille (lo-RAY)

eye
l'œil (LUH'yeh)

mouth
la bouche (boosh)

leg
la jambe (ZHAM-buh)

arm
le bras (brah)

hand
la main (man)

foot
le pied (pee-YAY)

6

7

Notes about the French language
The French use the vowel oe. The sound "oe" can change with each word. Look at the pronunciation for help to sound out each word.

The French language usually includes "la," "le" and "les" before nouns. These all mean "the" in French.
In French, "du" and "de la" mean some. The pronunciations for these articles are below.

| **la** (lah) | **les** (lay) | **de la** (duh lah) |
| **le** (luh) | **du** (dew) | |

uncle
l'oncle
(LONK-le)

mother
la mère
(mare)

cousin
le cousin
(coo-ZAN)

aunt
la tante
(tahnt)

baby
le bébé
(beh-BEH)

grandmother
la grand-mère
(grahnd-MARE)

father
le père
(pare)

grandfather
le grand-père
(grahnd-PARE)

sister
la sœur
(sur)

brother
le frère
(frare)

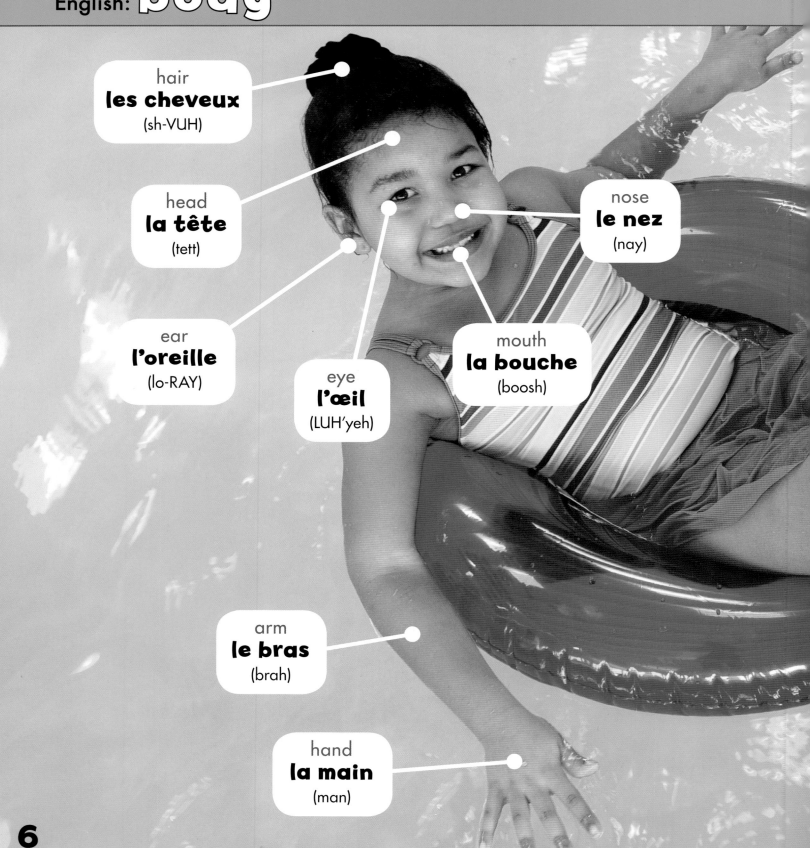

hair
les cheveux
(sh-VUH)

head
la tête
(tett)

nose
le nez
(nay)

ear
l'oreille
(lo-RAY)

eye
l'œil
(LUH'yeh)

mouth
la bouche
(boosh)

arm
le bras
(brah)

hand
la main
(man)

leg
la jambe
(ZHAM-buh)

foot
le pied
(pee-YAY)

pyjamas
le pyjama
(pee-zha-MAH)

coat
le manteau
(mahn-TOH)

shorts
le short
(short)

boot
la botte
(bott)

8

shoe
la chaussure
(show-SOOR)

hat
le chapeau
(sha-POH)

trousers
le pantalon
(pan-ta-LON)

sock
la chaussette
(show-SETT)

dress
la robe
(robe)

shirt
la chemise
(shuh-MEEZ)

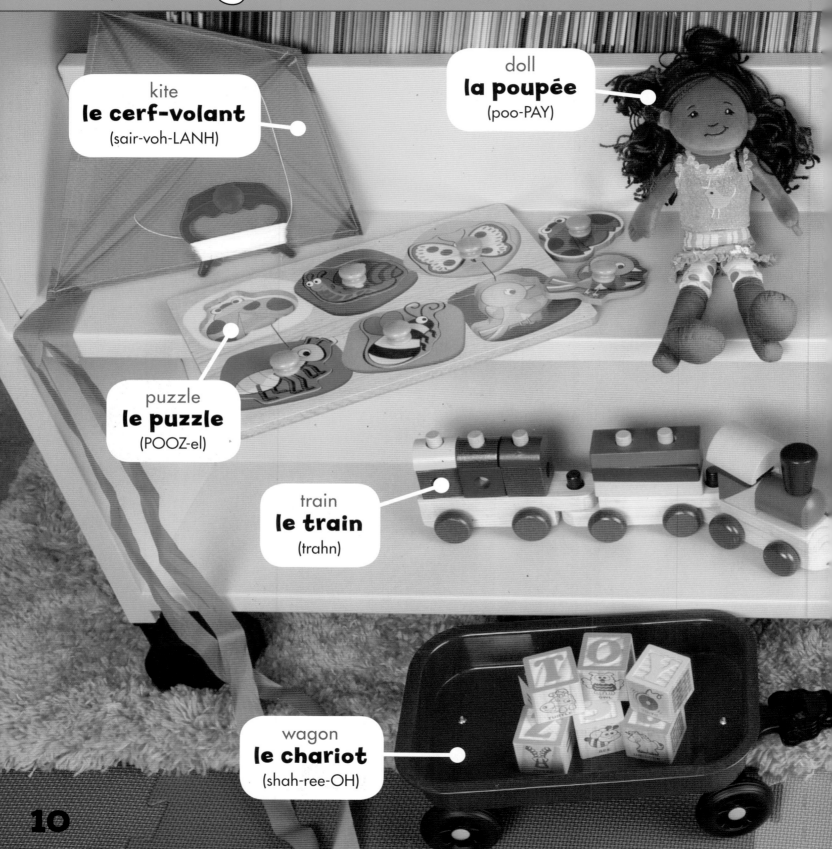

kite
le cerf-volant
(sair-voh-LANH)

doll
la poupée
(poo-PAY)

puzzle
le puzzle
(POOZ-el)

train
le train
(trahn)

wagon
le chariot
(shah-ree-OH)

puppet
la marionnette
(ma-ree-oh-NETT)

skateboard
le skateboard
(skayte-BORD)

skipping rope
la corde à sauter
(cord a soh-TAY)

ball
le ballon
(ba-LOHN)

bat
la batte
(baht)

11

picture
le tableau
(tah-BLOH)

lamp
la lampe
(lahmp)

window
la fenêtre
(fuh-NEH-trah)

chest of
drawers
la commode
(kum-MODE)

curtain
le rideau
(ree-DOH)

blanket
la couverture
(koo-ver-TUR)

French: **la chambre** (SHOM-brah)

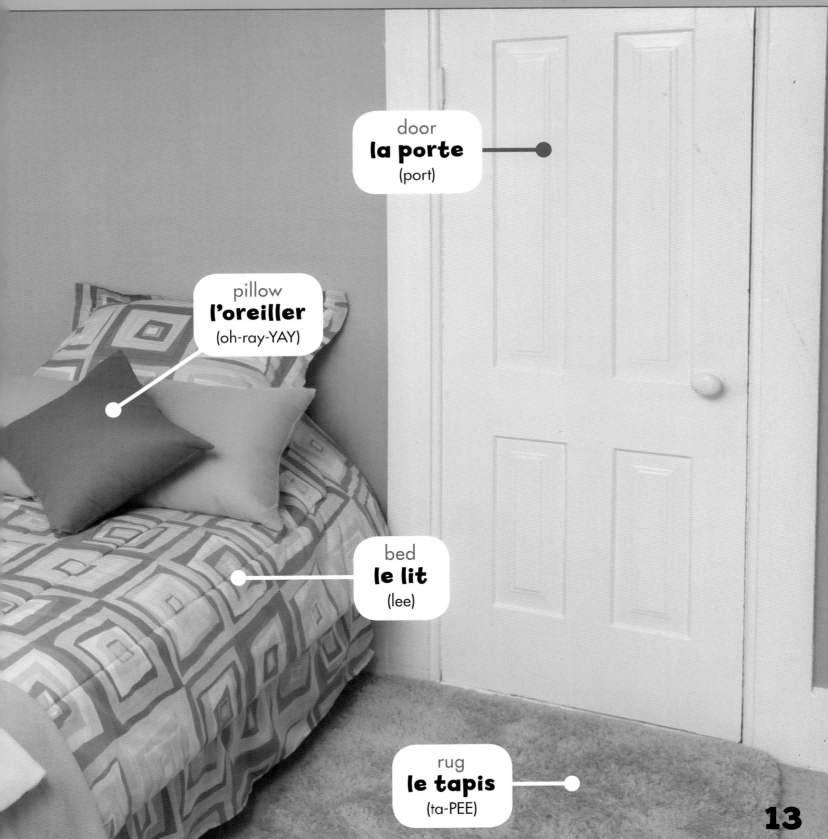

door
la porte
(port)

pillow
l'oreiller
(oh-ray-YAY)

bed
le lit
(lee)

rug
le tapis
(ta-PEE)

bath
la baignoire
(ban-WAHR)

soap
le savon
(sa-VOHN)

toilet
la toilette
(twa-LETT)

mirror
le miroir
(mee-RWAHR)

toothbrush
la brosse à dents
(bross a dahnt)

toothpaste
le dentifrice
(dahn-tee-FREECE)

comb
le peigne
(PAY-nye)

sink
le lavabo
(lah-vah-BOH)

towel
la serviette
(ser-vee-YETT)

brush
la brosse
(bross)

15

bowl
le bol
(bohl)

hob
la cuisinière
(kwee-zee-NYAYR)

pot
la marmite
(mar-MEET)

oven
le four
(foor)

16

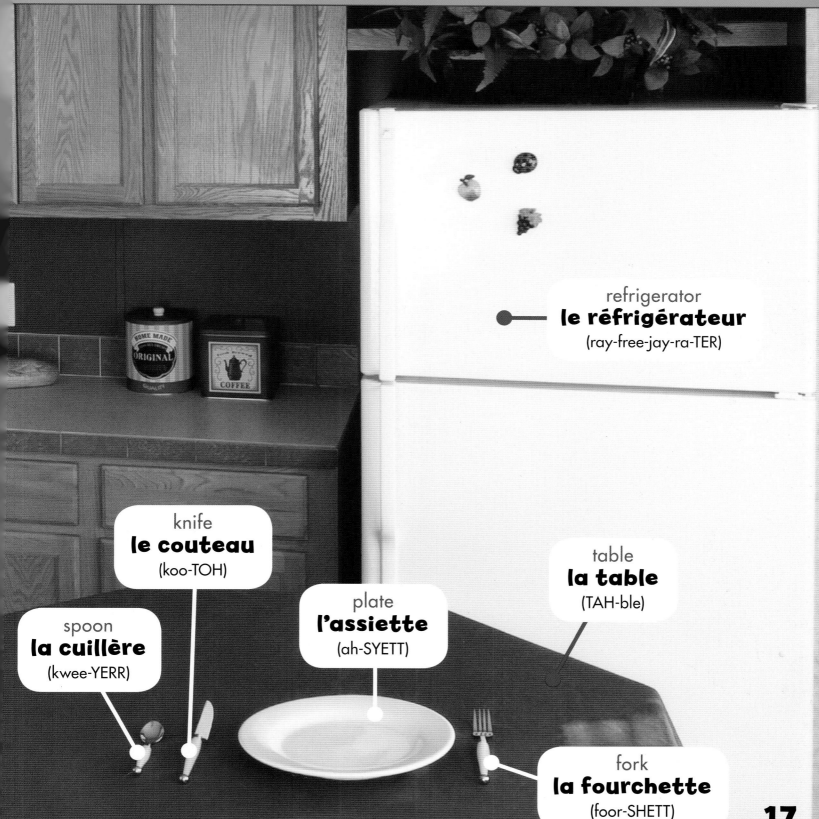

refrigerator
le réfrigérateur
(ray-free-jay-ra-TER)

knife
le couteau
(koo-TOH)

spoon
la cuillère
(kwee-YERR)

plate
l'assiette
(ah-SYETT)

table
la table
(TAH-ble)

fork
la fourchette
(foor-SHETT)

17

milk
du lait
(lay)

carrot
la carotte
(ka-ROTT)

bread
du pain
(pan)

apple
la pomme
(pom)

butter
du beurre
(buh-r)

egg
l'œuf
(uff)

pea
le pois
(pwa)

orange
l'orange
(o-RAHNZHE)

sandwich
le sandwich
(sahnd-WEECH)

rice
du riz
(ree)

19

tractor
le tracteur
(trak-TOOR)

hay
du foin
(fwahn)

fence
la clôture
(klo-TUR)

farmer
l'agriculteur
(ag-ree-kool-TOOR)

sheep
le mouton
(moo-TONH)

pig
le cochon
(koh-SHON)

20

horse
le cheval
(sh-VALL)

barn
la grange
(GRAN'zhe)

cow
la vache
(vash)

chicken
le poulet
(poo-LAY)

21

leaf
la feuille
(FEUY-ye)

butterfly
le papillon
(pa-pee-YON)

flower
la fleur
(flur)

trowel
la pelle
(pell)

bird
l'oiseau
(wa-ZOH)

worm
le ver
(ver)

22

plant
la plante
(plahnt)

grass
l'herbe
(lairb)

soil
de la terre
(tair)

seed
la graine
(grehnne)

23

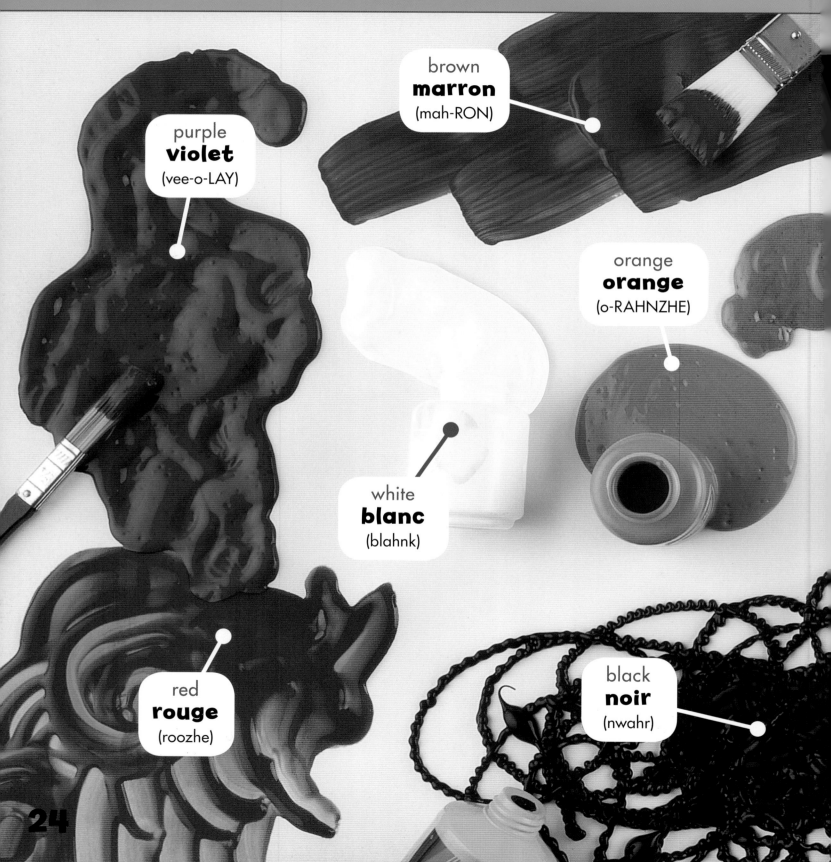

purple
violet
(vee-o-LAY)

brown
marron
(mah-RON)

orange
orange
(o-RAHNZHE)

white
blanc
(blahnk)

red
rouge
(roozhe)

black
noir
(nwahr)

24

pink
rose
(rohz)

blue
bleu
(bluh)

yellow
jaune
(zhohne)

green
vert
(verr)

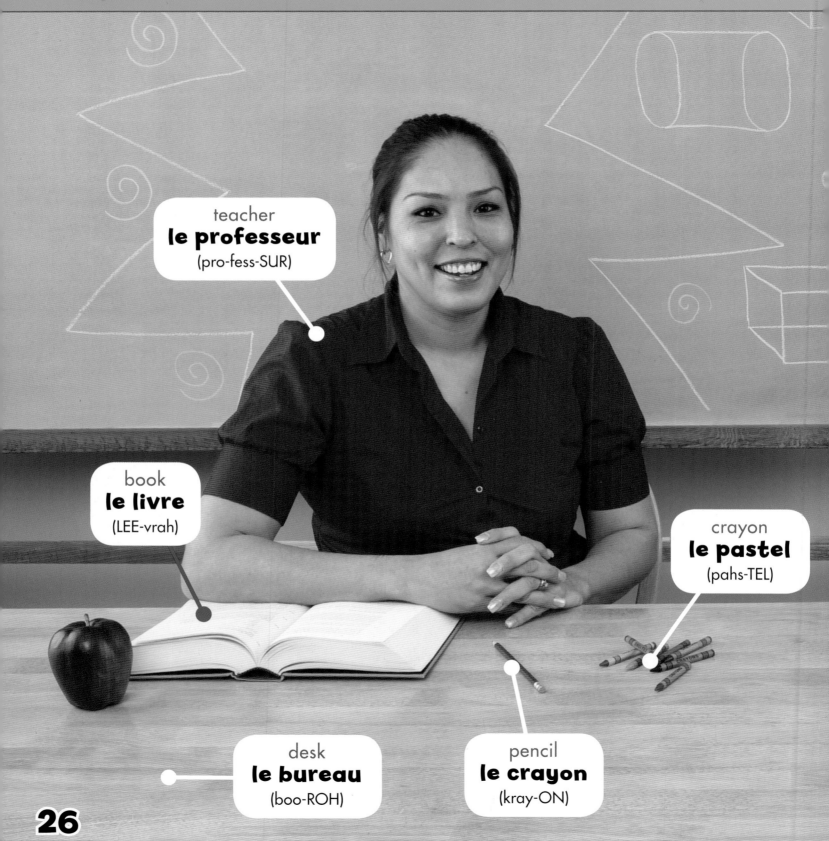

teacher
le professeur
(pro-fess-SUR)

book
le livre
(LEE-vrah)

crayon
le pastel
(pahs-TEL)

desk
le bureau
(boo-ROH)

pencil
le crayon
(kray-ON)

map
la carte
(cart)

clock
la pendule
(pahnd-DOOL)

computer
l'ordinateur
(or-din-a-TUR)

chair
la chaise
(shaize)

paper
le papier
(pa-pee-YAY)

traffic lights
les feux
(fuh)

library
la bibliothèque
(bib-lee-o-TEK)

shop
le magasin
(ma-ga-ZAHN)

bicycle
le vélo
(vay-LO)

car
la voiture
(vwa-TUR)

LIBRARY

ONE WAY

Tuesday 2:00-5:00
Thursday 2:00-6:00

tree
l'arbre
(AR-brah)

bus
l'autobus
(oh-to-BOOS)

park
le parc
(parc)

street
la rue
(roo)

sign
le panneau
(pahn-NOH)

STOP

29

Numbers • Les chiffres (SHEE-freh)

1. one • **un** (un)
2. two • **deux** (duh)
3. three • **trois** (twah)
4. four • **quatre** (KAT-trah)
5. five • **cinq** (sank)

6. six • **six** (seece)
7. seven • **sept** (sett)
8. eight • **huit** (weet)
9. nine • **neuf** (neuff)
10. ten • **dix** (deece)

Useful Phrases • Expressions utiles (ex-press-SYON oo-TEEL)

yes • **oui** (wee)

no • **non** (no'n)

hello • **bonjour** (bone-ZHOOR)

goodbye • **au revoir** (oh ruh-VWAR)

goodnight • **bonne nuit** (bunn NWEE)

please • **s'il vous plait** (see voo play)

thank you • **merci** (mer-SEE)

excuse me • **excusez-moi** (ex-KOO-zay-mwa)

My name is _____. • **Je m'appelle _____.** (zhe map-PEL)

Find out more

Look up more French words in these books:

Collins Very First French Dictionary (Collins, 2014)

My First Picture Dictionary: French/English, Isabel Carril (Wayland, 2008)

The Usborne Very First Dictionary in French, Felicity Brooks, Caroline Young, and Claire Masset (Usborne, 2008)

Websites

Visit these websites to learn more French words:

http://www.bbc.co.uk/schools/primarylanguages/french/

http://www.digitaldialects.com/French.htm

http://www.french-games.net/

Raintree is an imprint of Capstone Global Library Limited, a company incorporated in England and Wales having its registered office at 7 Pilgrim Street, London, EC4V 6LB – Registered company number: 6695582

www.raintree.co.uk
myorders@raintree.co.uk

Text © Capstone Global Library Limited 2015
First published in hardback in 2015
Paperback edition first published in 2016
The moral rights of the proprietor have been asserted.

Designed by Lori Bye
Picture research by Wanda Winch
Production by Eric Manske
Originated by Capstone Global Library Ltd
Printed and bound in China

ISBN 978 1 474 70686 5 (hardback)
19 18 17 16
10 9 8 7 6 5 4 3 2 1

ISBN 978 1 474 70692 6 (paperback)
20 19 18 17 16
10 9 8 7 6 5 4 3 2 1

British Library Cataloguing in Publication Data
A full catalogue record for this book is available from the British Library.

Acknowledgements
We would like to thank the following for permission to reproduce photographs: Capstone Press/Gary Sundermeyer, cover (pig), 20 (farmer with tractor, pig); Capstone Press/Karon Dubke, cover (ball, sock), back cover (toothbrush, apple), 1, 3, 4–5, 6–7, 8–9, 10–11, 12–13, 14–15, 16–17, 18–19, 22–23, 24–25, 26–27; Image Farm, back cover, 1, 2, 31, 32 (design elements); iStockphoto/Andrew Gentry, 28 (main street); Photodisc, cover (flower); Shutterstock/Adrian Matthiassen, cover (butterfly); David Hughes, 20 (hay); Eric Isselee, 20–21 (horse); hamurishi, 28 (bike); Jim Mills, 29 (stop sign); Kelli Westfal, 28 (traffic light); Levgeniia Tikhonova, 21 (chickens); Margo Harrison, 20 (sheep); MaxPhoto, 21 (cow and calf); Melinda Fawver, 29 (bus); Robert Elias, 20–21 (barn, fence); Vladimir Mucibabic, 28–29 (city skyline).

Every effort has been made to contact copyright holders of material reproduced in this book. Any omissions will be rectified in subsequent printings if notice is given to the publisher.

All the internet addresses (URLs) given in this book were valid at the time of going to press. However, due to the dynamic nature of the internet, some addresses may have changed, or sites may have changed or ceased to exist since publication. While the author and publisher regret any inconvenience this may cause readers, no responsibility for any such changes can be accepted by either the author or the publisher.

Note to parents, teachers and librarians
Learning to speak a second language at a young age has been shown to improve overall academic performance, boost problem-solving ability and foster an appreciation for other cultures. Early exposure to language skills provides a strong foundation for other subject areas, including maths and reasoning. Introducing children to a second language can help to lay the groundwork for future academic success and cultural awareness.